Circles of Grace

Worship *and* Prayer *in the* Everyday

Keri K. Wehlander

The United Church Publishing House

Quiltmaker God,
with wise and holy patience
you caress delicate threads
remembering every story,
each detail,
as you hum new patterns.

The rhythm of your love
braids together
patches, pieces, tints and textures,
scattered odds and separate ends,
weaving and spinning
and shaping them into a dappled unity.

Resting for a moment,
you contemplate this creation,
aware of each tear, every stable seam,
the intricacies of the whole.

Gently, you gather us up,
this crazy quilt that we are,
and you call us good once more.

Circles of Grace
Worship and Prayer in the Everyday

All biblical quotations are adapted from either *The New Oxford Annotated Bible with the Apocrypha*, New Revised Standard Version, Bruce M. Metzger and Roland E. Murphy, eds., (New York: Oxford University Press, 1991), or *The New Jerusalem Bible* (Garden City, N.Y.: Darton, Longman & Todd/Doubleday & Co., 1985).

Canadian Cataloguing in Publication Data

Wehlander, Keri, 1956-
Circles of Grace : worship and prayer in the everyday

Includes index.
ISBN 1-55134-080-1

1. Worship programs. I. Title.

BV198.W43 1998 264 C98-930506-6

United Church Publishing House
3250 Bloor Street West, Fourth Floor
Etobicoke, Ontario
Canada M8X 2Y4
(416) 231-5931
bookpub@uccan.org
www.uccan.org/ucph

Editing, design and production: Department of Publishing and Graphics
Cover image: Dresden Plate pattern, Mennonite quilt from Kitchener, Ontario

Printed in Canada

 980038

Circles of Grace

Contents

Kim Denae Wehlander

"My heart remembers"

Preface

At the heart of this book is a desire for worship and prayer to be accessible enough to become part of the rhythm of daily life. Our deep yearning for moments that we call "holy" can certainly come in those unexpected experiences that inspire and astound us. But this yearning also is met through our acknowledgment of the immediacy of God's presence in common, everyday moments. At best, prayer and worship enable us to do just that. At worst, these practices become enslaved by rule and rubric, and thereby create a sense of distance from all that is holy. When we look at the root of the word "worship," we find the Anglo-Saxon word, *weorthscipe,* which means "worth-ship." Thus, through this experience, we should be able to proclaim the worth of God in our lives, as well as seeing the intrinsic worth of our own lives and of this world we are a part of.

Underlying prayer and worship are two very simple qualities: opening space and opening our spirits. In opening a space, we are intentionally setting time and place apart to be with God. In opening our spirits, we are listening deeply to what our own hearts wish to say, as well as listening for the heartbeat of God's presence. This means that we may express gratitude, concern, anger, ask questions, or simply sit in silence. As we listen, we may have a shift in perception, a moment of tranquility, a sense of commitment, or the gift of a moment of stillness. Whatever the experience, we trust that our relationship with God will deepen.

With these reflections in mind, it is my hope that *Circles of Grace* will serve as an encouragement to any individuals, groups or families who feel drawn to prayer and worship in their lives. Remember that the worship we have become familiar with began as simple and informal at-home gatherings of small groups or families to pray, pass along stories, celebrate communion and support one another in the journey of faith.

In closing, I offer some words of thanks. Following the publication of *Joy is our Banquet*, many people shared stories with me of where and how the services were used, and expressed appreciation for them. Others encouraged me to write more of this kind of material, and made specific suggestions. Many thanks to all of you. I hope that you will enjoy this book, and know that you played a part in it being written. Thanks to those at the United Church Publishing House and Department of Publishing and Graphics who offered encouragement and expertise in bringing *Circles of Grace* to print.

A final word of love and thanks goes to Curtis Aguirre, from whom I have certainly received grace after grace.

Keri K. Wehlander
Burnaby, British Columbia
January 1998

Celebrating God's Presence

Intricate Wonders

Gathering

One: Intricate wonders adorn our days,
Bidding us to consider them
With grateful eyes.

All: **May our living sing praise to you, O God.**

One: Each lifetime permeated with quiet sacraments
Offered in common encounters,
Yet reflecting celestial light.

All: **May our living sing praise to you, O God.**

One: This banquet of humble mysteries
Nourishes our spirit's yearning
If we would be still and receive.

All: **May our living sing praise to you, O God.**

Song: For the Beauty of the Earth

Readings

Psalm 96:1, 3, 11-12, 4

O sing to God a new song; sing all the earth! Declare God's glory among the nations, and God's marvelous works among all the peoples. Let the heavens be glad, and let the earth rejoice; let the sea roar, and all that fills it; let the field exult, and everything in it... For great is God, and greatly to be praised.

Exodus 3:1-3a, 5

Moses... led his flock beyond the wilderness, and came to Horeb, the mountain of God. There the angel of God appeared to him in a flame of fire out of a bush; he looked, and the bush was blazing, yet it was not consumed. Then Moses said, "I must turn aside and look at this great sight" ... and God called to Moses, "Remove the sandals from your feet, for the place on which you are standing is holy ground."

Luke 1:46-47, 49

And Mary said, "My soul magnifies God, in whom my spirit finds joy... for the Mighty One has done great things for me, and holy is God's name."

Sirach 43:9-12, 17b-19, 23, 25-27

The glory of the stars is the beauty of heaven, a glittering array in the heights of God. At God's word they stand in their appointed places... Look at the rainbow... it is exceedingly beautiful in its brightness. It encircles the sky with its glorious arc; the hands of the Most High have stretched it out... God scatters the snow like birds flying down... The eye is dazzled by the beauty of its whiteness, and the mind is amazed as it falls. God pours frost over the earth like salt, and icicles form like pointed thorns... God stilled the deep and planted islands in it... It is filled with strange and marvelous creatures, all kinds of life... By God's word all things hold together. We could say more but could never say enough; let the final word be: "God is all."

Response

Prayer of Wonder

To witness an ebony quilt of sky
stitched by beaming stars;
And awaken to ancient cedar's sway
dancing with the wind,
Is to glimpse God's scattering of grace.

To recognize an inner flutter and pulse
as new life's movement in the womb;
Or hear a tone so sweetly sung
that heaven opens within,
Is to stand at the threshold of everything holy.

To wonder at the sweep of a whale
breaching the air from concealed depths;
Or gaze at the ripples and curves formed above
by a cloud of wings on the move,
Is to be breathless with praise for the radiance of life.

Song: Joyful, Joyful We Adore You

Prayer Walk

Preparation: *The worship space needs to be set up with four separate stations for prayer: Discernment; Healing; Thanksgiving; and Resting in God. One possibility is to place these stations in the four corners of the room. Chairs, matches, votive candles, and a container of sand to place candles in needs to be at each station. A banner or piece of art pertaining to the focus of each station may be added. Chairs need to be placed in the middle of the worship space for the beginning and ending of the service, and so that participants can choose to walk to the stations when they feel ready.*

Gathering

One: Come, all those weary
From the crowd and bustle of the day:

All: **God's steadfast love awaits you.**

One: Come, all those with delight
For the abundance of everyday treasures:

All: **God's steadfast love awaits you.**

One: Come, all those made restless
By acquiescence to injustice:

All: **God's steadfast love awaits you.**

One: Come, all those who search
For glimpses of quiet transcendence:

All: **God's steadfast love awaits you.**

One: Come, all those with spirits frayed
From the pull of unforeseen difficulties:

All: **God's steadfast love awaits you.**

One: Come, all those with open hearts
Ready to listen for the mystery:

All: **God's steadfast love awaits you.**

Time of Singing: Jubilate Deo; God Is the One Whom We Seek Together; Gloria; Send Your Holy Spirit

Prayer Walk

Participants are invited to walk to the stations they wish to pray at as they feel ready. Scripture passages are provided on each of the chairs. At each station, participants are invited to light a candle, and place it in the sand as a sign of their petitions. Quiet instrumental music would enhance this time of prayer.

Readings

Discernment

Psalm 119:105

Your word is a lamp to my feet and a light to my path.

Healing

Psalm 36:7

How precious is your steadfast love, O God!
All people may take refuge in the shelter of your wings.

Thanksgiving

Psalm 66:1, 98:1

Make a joyful noise, all the earth;
for God has done marvelous things.

Resting in God

Psalm 139:1-3

O God, you have searched me and known me. You know when I sit down and when I rise up; you discern my thoughts from far away. You search out my path... and are acquainted with all my ways.

Response

Song: O God We Call; or Kindle a Flame to Lighten the Dark

Prayer

Holy One,

With gentle hands

Receive our prayers.

With patient eyes

Search out our spirits.

With quiet words

Offer us peace.

With your infinite heart

Receive our lives.

Amen.

Time of Singing: Come, Holy Spirit; Nothing Can Trouble

Blessing

May mercy be our path

And peace fill all our days

May love heal every heart

And God's grace light our way.

Amen.

Circles of Grace

Gathering

One: Renewing Spirit,

We come in weariness and with unwrapped wounds,

Seeking a patient compassion.

All: **As the waters which colour dry lands into greening,**

So may we be renewed by your touch.

One: Gentling Spirit,

As dilemmas and demands confound us,

We long for unexpected tenderness.

All: **As the breeze caresses fields of grain into ripples,**

So may we be gentled by your touch.

One: Transforming Spirit,

Diminished by the practice of malice,

We dream of a common righteousness.

All: **As the fiery burst of sun through clouds,**
So may we be transformed by your touch.

One: Quieting Spirit,
In our crowded hours and paths,
We yearn for an interior peace.

All: **As the soil embraces each seed seeking growth,**
So may we be quieted by your touch.
Amen.

Song: In the Quiet Curve of Evening

Readings

Luke 17:20-21
Once Jesus was asked by the Pharisees when the realm of God was coming, and he answered... "the realm of God is already in your midst."

Genesis 28:11-16
Jacob came to a certain place and stayed there for the night, because the sun had set. Taking one of the stones of the place, he put it under his head and lay down in that place And he dreamed that there was a stairway set up on the earth, the top of it reaching to heaven; and the angels of God were ascending and descending on it. And God stood beside him and said, "I am the God of Abraham and Sarah, and of Rebekah and Isaac, your ancestors. The land on which you lie I will give to you and to your offspring... and all the families of the earth shall be blessed in you and in your offspring.

Know that I am with you and will keep you wherever you go, and will bring you back to this land..." And Jacob woke from his sleep and said, "Surely God is in this place — and I did not know it!"

Ephesians 3:16-19
I pray that... you may be strengthened in your inner being with power through the Spirit, and that Christ may dwell in your hearts through faith, as you are being rooted and grounded in love. I pray that you may have the power to comprehend, with all the saints... the breadth and length and height and depth... of the love of Christ... so that you may be filled with all the fullness of God.

Luke 1:39-45
In those days Mary set out and went with haste to a Judean town in the hill country, where she entered the house of Zechariah and Elizabeth. When Elizabeth heard Mary's greeting, the child leaped in her womb. And Elizabeth was filled with the Holy Spirit and exclaimed with a loud cry, "Blessed are you among women, and blessed is the child of your womb!"

John 1:16
...we have all received grace upon grace.

Prayer

Holy One:

We live at mystery's edge,

Watching for a startling luminescence

Or a word to guide us.

In fragile occurrences

You present yourself

And we must pause to meet you.

Daily, there are glimmers,

Reflections of a seamless mercy

Revealed in common intricacies.

These circles of grace

Spill out around us

And announce that we are a part of you.

Amen.

Song: God of the Sparrow

DAILY DISCERNINGS

Preparation for Daily Prayer

In each of these services of prayer for individual use, you may find some of the following suggestions helpful to you.

Locate a place where you can be comfortably seated, with both feet on the ground. Often, a focal point placed on a table in front of you can make your environment feel prayerful. Possibilities for this might include: a special tapestry or cloth, flowers, an icon or a depiction of a Biblical story, a photograph, a basket, a Bible, a painting or carving, a bowl of water, incense, a special stone, or lit candles. Another possibility might be to play music that you find to be meditative and meaningful in the background. In creating time and space for prayer, simply be aware of what elements make you feel focused, comfortable and connected to what is holy.

With each of these services, take some time at the beginning to create a sense of relaxation in your body. You can do this with a few gentle stretches and some slow, deep breaths.

As you enter into a time of prayer, be patient with yourself. Remember that the idea behind each of these services is quite simple: prayer is a time of paying attention to one's relationship with God.

God's Song

A service of prayer for the individual

Time of Preparation

Centering Prayer

In this moment, O God,

I turn to you.

May my ebb and flow of thinking

Settle into stillness.

May each heaviness I carry

Be released into your love.

May the cycles of my breathing

Restore a spaciousness within.

May I listen gently enough

To touch the hem of your presence.

Amen.

Readings

Isaiah 43:1, 4a, 5a
Thus says the God who formed and created you: "Do not fear, for I have redeemed you; I have called you by name, you are mine... You are precious in my sight, and honoured, and I love you... Do not fear, for I am with you."

Jeremiah 17:7-8
Blessed are those who trust in God, whose trust is our God. They shall be like a tree planted by water, sending out its roots by the stream. When the heat comes, there is nothing to fear, and its leaves shall stay green; in the year of drought it is not anxious, and it does not cease to bear fruit.

Micah 6:8
What does God require of you, but to act with justice, to love kindness, and to walk humbly with your God?

Philippians 4:8
Finally, beloved, whatever is true, whatever is honorable, whatever is just, whatever is pure, whatever is pleasing, whatever is commendable, if there is any excellence and if there is anything worthy of praise, think about these things.

Prayer for Reflection

Holy One,

Like light spilling through dappled trees,

You are with me.

Like wind rippling through curtained windows,

You are with me.

Like water ever smoothing the sandy beach,

You are with me.

Embraced by your presence,

I open my heart to you.

Encouraged by your love,

I release my thoughts to you.

Intrigued by your mysteries,

I listen now for your song.

Amen.

Silent Reflection

Blessing

In each breath this day, may there be peace.

In each step this day, may there be grace.

In each word this day, may there be compassion.

In each encounter this day, may God's presence be known.

Amen.

A Turning Season

Prayer of discernment for the individual

Time of Preparation

In preparation for this service, you may wish to place two small pieces of paper in front of you — one left blank, and one with your current concern written on it. A pen or pencil nearby would also be helpful.

Prayer

God, my Source of Strength:
A season is turning in my life
Calling me to make ready:
Walk with me, I pray.

This unmapped course lies divided ahead
Urging careful determination:
Walk with me, I pray.

The gate has swung open and everything's loose

Bidding that something be left behind:

Walk with me, I pray.

Until the turbulent waters clear

I reach for your mercy

and pray for wisdom:

Walk with me, I pray.

Amen.

Readings

Psalm 143:8, 10
O God, let me hear of your steadfast love in the morning, for in you I put my trust. Teach me the way I should go, for to you I lift up my soul... You are my God: Let your good spirit lead me on a level path.

1 Corinthians 13:12
For now we see in a mirror, dimly, but then we will see face to face. Now I know only in part; then I will know fully, even as I have been fully known. And now, faith, hope and love abide, these three; and the greatest of these is love.

Jeremiah 6:16
Stand at the crossroads and look, and ask for the ancient paths, where the good way lies; and walk in it, and find rest for your souls.

2 Samuel 22:33-34
God has girded me with strength and has opened wide my path. God has made my feet like the feet of the deer, and has set me secure on the heights.

John 14:27
Peace I leave with you; my peace I give to you. I do not give to you as the world gives. Do not let your hearts be troubled, and do not let them be afraid.

Silent Reflection

If a word or image comes to you during this time, you may wish to record it on the blank piece of paper in front of you, and carry it with you as a reminder through the day.

Prayer for the Journey

God of Blessing,

With pilgrim's feet

I trace this fresh journey

One step at a time.

With an apprentice's regard

I seek a clear vision

One landscape at a time.

With a dancer's heart
I trust the centre to hold
One leap at a time.

With a mother's tender arms
You cradle my new spirit
One breath at a time.
Amen.

Light of Healing

Prayer of healing for the individual

Time of Preparation

Centering Prayer

Holy One,

Light of all healing:

Be present with me.

Rooted in your love,

May I be.

Filled with your peace,

May I be.

Illumined by your grace,

May I be.

Kindle my heart

into quiet strength.

Calm my spirit

into restoration.

Touch my life

into wholeness again.

Amen.

Readings

Psalm 57:1
Be merciful to me, O God... for in you my soul takes refuge; in the shadow of your wings I will take refuge from the storm.

Prayer

Holy One,

Light of all healing:

Be my shelter,

Be my strength.

Isaiah 54:10
For the mountains may depart and the hills be removed, but my steadfast love shall not depart from you, and my covenant of peace shall not be removed, says God, who has compassion on you.

Prayer

Holy One,

Light of all healing:

Hold me in your steadfast love

As I face ... *(individual's concern is named)*

May I rest in your compassion.

May I know your peace.

Isaiah 58:8
Your light shall break forth like the dawn, and your healing shall rise up in you.

Prayer

Holy One,

Light of all healing

Renew and sustain me

Like the shining of the dawn.

Amen.

Time for Silent Reflection

Prayer of Blessing

In this day's journey,
life blessing moments.

In this day's journey,
a peaceful spirit.

In this day's journey,
words which strengthen.

In this day's journey,
God's healing love.
Amen.

New Light

Morning prayer for those with busy schedules

Time of Preparation

Prayer

In the shelter of new light
Before day's weight begins
O God, hear my prayer.

As earth charts her course towards night
So may I chart mine:
with quiet clarity,
with visible compassion,
with clear integrity.

May the scope of this created journey
Run broad with recognition:
for each subtle miracle,

for each transparent mercy,
for each tender joy.

May the sweep of this day be steadied
By your gestures of presence:
Infectious grace,
Persistent love,
Outrageous vision;
Until an iridescence grows within
Marking my course with peaceful certainty.
Amen.

Readings

Lamentations 3:22-23
The steadfast love of God never ceases; God's mercies never come to an end; they are new every morning.

Psalm 139:9-10
If I take the wings of the morning and settle at the farthest limits of the sea, even there your hand shall lead me...

Psalm 118:24
This is the day that God has made; let us rejoice and be glad in it.

Blessing

Holy One:

Breathing in your spacious peace,
I welcome this day.

Resting in your expansive love,
I welcome this day.

Trusting in your perpetual hope,
I welcome this day.

Living in your created image,
I welcome this day.
Amen.

Seeking Transformation

Dancing into Freedom

Gathering

One: In daily patterns and settings
We travel well-worn paths,
We learn conventional ways,
We surrender to how it has always been.

All: **Dance us into freedom, O Cloud and Flame of Life.**

One: We prioritize perceived expectations,
We neglect our uncommon dreams,
We shape our lives with fear and familiarity.

All: **Dance us into freedom, O Cloud and Flame of Life.**

One: We claim not to see the corruptions,
We protect common myths with our lies,
We perjure the gospel within us.

All: **Dance us into freedom, O Cloud and Flame of Life.**

One: We confine the breadth of our choices,
We deny the depth of our hopes,
We limit the strength of our lives.

All: **Dance us into freedom, O Cloud and Flame of Life.**

Song: Will You Come and Follow Me

Readings

John 8:31-32
Then Jesus said... "If you continue in my word, you are truly my disciples; and you will know the truth, and the truth will set you free."

Romans 12:1a, 2
I urge you, then, brothers and sisters, remembering the mercies of God... Do not be conformed to this world, but be transformed by the renewing of your minds, so that you may discern what is the will of God.

Exodus 13:21-22; 14:21-22; 15:19-20

God went in front of the people of Israel in a pillar of cloud by day, to lead them along the way, and in a pillar of fire by night to give them light, so that they might travel by day and by night. Neither the pillar of cloud by day nor the pillar of fire by night left its place in front of the people... When the people reached the sea, Moses stretched his hand out over it. God drove the sea back by a strong east wind all night, and turned the sea into dry land; and the waters were divided. The Israelites went into the sea on dry ground, the waters forming a wall for them on their right and their left... When the Pharaoh with his chariots and his chariot drivers went into the sea in pursuit of the Israelites... the waters of the sea closed once again; but the Israelites walked through the sea on dry ground. Then the prophet Miriam... took a tambourine in her hand; and all the women went out after her with tambourines and with dancing.

Galatians 5:1

For freedom Christ has set us free. Stand firm, therefore, and do not submit again to a yoke of slavery.

A Prayer for Daring

Unfettered God:

This journey of living

is meant for daring, not slavery.

Release the courage within, we pray.

These worlds we are creating

must proclaim vision, not contempt.

Awaken the strength of our wisdom, we pray.

These hearts that beat within us

are created for mystery, not diminishment.

Free the splendor of your hope, we pray.

This faith that we carry

calls for liberation, not inertia.

Clear a path for your spirit within us, we pray.

Amen.

Song: Lead On, O Cloud of Presence

To Dare Rebirth

Preparation: *Candles are needed for each person present to light at the end of the service. Three candles are needed in the middle of the circle. They are lit at the beginning of the service, are blown out one by one where indicated, and then relit one by one in the Readings section.*

Gathering

One: Invisible manuals of power

Divide us, and call for subtraction.

All: **The angels cry with each new birth,**

"May good will reign, may peace prevail."

One: Relentless vehicles of intolerance

Permeate our patterns of choice.

All: **The angels cry with each new birth,**

"May good will reign, may peace prevail."

One: Distorted windows of economy

Render lives into chaff.

All: **The angels cry with each new birth,**

"May good will reign, may peace prevail."

One: Arrogant storehouses of violence

Poison the web of life.

All: **The angels cry with each new birth,**

"May good will reign, may peace prevail."

Song: He Came Singing Love

Readings

GENESIS 4:8-9

Cain said to his brother Abel, "Let us go out to the field." And when they were in the field, Cain rose up against his brother Abel, and killed him. Then God said to Cain, "Where is your brother?" And Cain said, "I do not know; am I my brother's keeper?"

Reader blows out a candle in middle of circle.

EZEKIEL 22:25

The rulers within your land are like roaring lions tearing the prey; they have destroyed human lives; they have taken treasure and precious things; they have made many widows within it. The priests of your land have done violence to my teaching and have profaned that which is holy... The officials within your land are like wolves tearing the prey, shedding blood, destroying lives to get dishonest gain. Your prophets have smeared whitewash on their behalf, seeing false visions and divining lies, saying, "Thus says God," when God has not spoken. The people of the land have practiced extortion and committed robbery; they have oppressed the poor and needy, and have extorted from the stranger without redress.

Reader blows out a candle in middle of circle.

Matthew 2:16-18
When Herod saw that he had been tricked by the wise men, he was infuriated, and he sent and killed all the children in and around Bethlehem who were two years old or under... Then was fulfilled what had been spoken through the prophet Jeremiah: "A voice was heard in Ramah, wailing and loud lamentation, Rachel weeping for her children; she refused to be consoled, because they are no more."

Reader blows out a candle in middle of circle.

Song: Kindle a Flame to Lighten the Dark

Ezekiel 11:19
Thus says our God: "I will give you a new heart, and put a new spirit within you."

Reader lights a candle in middle of circle.

Song: Kindle a Flame to Lighten the Dark

Revelation 21:1
Then I saw a new heaven and a new earth; for the first heaven and the first earth had passed away... And I heard a loud voice... saying, "See, the home of God is among the peoples. God will dwell with them... and will wipe every tear from their eyes."

Reader lights a candle in middle of circle.

Song: Kindle a Flame to Lighten the Dark

John 3:1-5
Now there was a Pharisee named Nicodemus, a leader of the Jews. He came to Jesus by night and said to him, "Rabbi, we know that

you are a teacher who has come from God; for no one can do these signs that you do apart from the presence of God." Jesus answered him, "Very truly, I tell you, no one can see the realm of God without being born from above." Nicodemus said to him, "How can anyone be born after having grown old? Can one enter a second time into the mother's womb and be born? Jesus answered, "Very truly, I tell you... you must be born of the Spirit."

Reader lights a candle in middle of circle.

Song: Kindle a Flame to Lighten the Dark

Prayer for Rebirth

That we might dare rebirth:

Leaving behind

all the ransomed exchanges,

all the narrow corruptions,

all the familiar betrayals.

That we might dare rebirth:

Allowing the breadth of love to give us life,

the depth of justice to rhythm our hearts,

the height of peace to nourish our days.

That we might dare rebirth:

Shaping a world that welcomes gentleness,

a world that dances with joy,

a world where God is at rest;

A world shaped not simply for ourselves,

but for all living yet to come.

Each person is invited to light a candle and place it in the middle of the circle as a prayer for rebirth in their own lives, and in our world.

Song: O for a World

Shake the Foundations

Preparation: *Enough good sized stones with smooth surfaces and felt markers for each person present.*

Gathering

One: When greed shapes the walls of our structures,
When callousness hinges the doors of decision:

All: **Let the foundations be shaken and God's realm begun!**

One: When ruthlessness reigns in the stairwells of power,
When deception is basic because control is the key:

All: **Let the foundations be shaken and God's realm begun!**

One: When prejudice is stored in our hallways of habit,
When denial shelters the hearth of our fears:

All: Let the foundations be shaken and God's realm begun!

Song: Live into Hope

Readings

Amos 5:21-24

I hate, I despise your festivals, and I take no delight in your solemn assemblies. Even though you bring your offerings... I will not accept them... I will not look upon them. Take away from me the noise of your songs; I will not listen to the melody of your harps. But let justice roll down like waters, and righteousness like an ever-flowing stream.

Jeremiah 6:13-15

From the least to the greatest of them, everyone is greedy for unjust gain; and from prophet to priest, everyone deals falsely. They have treated the wound of my people carelessly, saying, "Peace, peace," when there is no peace. They acted shamefully, they committed abomination; yet they were not ashamed."

Isaiah 43:18-19

Thus says our God, "Do not remember the former things or consider the things of old. I am about to do a new thing; now it springs forth, do you not perceive it?"

Isaiah 40:4-5

Every valley shall be lifted up, and every mountain and hill be made low; the uneven ground shall become level, and the rough places a plain. Then the glory of God shall be revealed, and all people shall see it together.

Matthew 20:16
So the last will be first, and the first will be last.

Acts 17:6
And they dragged some of the believers before the city authorities, shouting, "These people who are turning the world upside down have come here also!"

Psalm 118:22-23
The stone that the builders rejected has become the chief cornerstone. This is God's doing; it is marvelous in our eyes.

Response

Cornerstone Reflection

Each person is given a good sized stone with smooth surfaces, and a felt marker. They are invited to write a word/phrase on the stone the reflects an element they would like to see valued at the foundations of our society/church. When all have finished, each person is invited to share their "cornerstone" with the rest of the group, and place it in the middle of the circle.

Song: I See a New Heaven

Prayer

Unsettling God,

Dizzy with your vision,

May we craft our living

With realized mercies

And unfashionable hope.

Transformed by your message,
May we disrupt idolatrous norms
With the vigor of justice
And the plain language of faith.

Resolute in your embrace,
May we form new foundations
With the endurance of love
And a passion for grace.
Amen.

Song of Blessing: When You Walk from Here

Rejoicing With Children

A Child is Given

To welcome a new baby or child into the family

Gathering

One: Like day's first light,
This new life is promise and mystery.

All: **Child of grace and wonder —**
We welcome you,
We share our love for you.

One: Like a chorus of songbirds,
This new life is joy and celebration.

All: **Child of grace and wonder —**
We welcome you,
We share our love for you.

One: Like spring's fragrant bouquet,
This new life is beauty and tenderness.

All: **Child of grace and wonder —**

We welcome you,

We share our love for you.

One: Like earth's rhythm of abundance,

This new life is gift and treasure.

All: **Child of grace and wonder —**

We welcome you,

We share our love for you.

Song: Mothering God, You Gave Me Birth

Readings

Luke 1:57-58

Now the time came for Elizabeth to give birth and she bore a son. When her neighbors and relatives heard this... they came and rejoiced with Elizabeth and Zechariah.

Psalm 139:13-14

For it was you who formed me; you knit me together in my mother's womb. I praise you, O God, for I am fearfully and wonderfully made. Wonderful are your works; that I know very well.

Matthew 18:1-2, 4-5

The disciples came to Jesus and asked, "Who is the greatest in the realm of heaven?" And Jesus called a child, whom he put among them, and said... "Whoever becomes... like this child is the greatest in the realm of heaven. Whoever welcomes one such child in my name welcomes me."

Response

Through the sharing of stories, photographs and readings, the new child is celebrated and welcomed. Those present at the birth or adoption may wish to share the story of that experience. The name of the child may be honoured with stories of how it was chosen, and those gathered might wish to bring poems and stories that use the child's name.

Blessing

All: **May your journey in life**
Shine with a star's delight.

May your days and your years
Weave together a wondrous tapestry.

May your unfolding story
Dance with the grace of every blessing.

Always and ever, may you rest in God.
Always and ever, may God rest in you.
Amen.

God Welcomes Us

A service to introduce children to the rhythm of worship

We Greet God

The following gestures may be used with the phrases which suggest them: hands on heart, walking in place and giving a small jump in the air.

One: With a heart of love

All: **With a heart of love**

One: God welcomes us.

All: **God welcomes us.**

One: With a word of hope

All: **With a word of hope**

One: God walks with us.

All: **God walks with us.**

One: With a jump for joy

All: **With a jump for joy**

One: God gives thanks for ***(each participant calls out their name).***

One: With a heart of love

All: **With a heart of love**

One: We welcome God.

All: **We welcome God.**

One: With a word of hope

All: **With a word of hope**

One: We walk with God.

All: **We walk with God.**

One: With a jump for joy

All: **With a jump for joy**

One: We give thanks to God!

All: **We give thanks to God!**

Song: Praise Our Maker; or Jesus Loves Me; or For All Your Goodness, God; or What Does the Lord Require of You; or any other songs familiar to you and the children.

We Listen to Stories of God

You may wish to read one or more of these passages, and then read a story from a children's Bible. Some suggestions: Creation (Genesis 1:1-2:4); The Flood and the Rainbow (Genesis 6:14-9:17); God Feeds the People in the Wilderness (Exodus 16); Jesus' story of the Good Samaritan (Luke 10:25-37); A Child helps Jesus to Feed a Crowd (John 6:1-14); Jesus Heals a Bent Over Woman (Luke 13:10-17).

Psalm 47:1
Clap your hands, all you peoples; shout to God with songs of joy!

Psalm 150:6
Let everything that breathes praise God!

Matthew 19:14
And Jesus said, "Let the children come to me... for the realm of heaven belongs to them."

1 John 4:16b
God is love, and whoever lives in love lives in God and God lives in them.

We Share in God's Blessing

Blessing

Each gesture is held for two lines, and is repeated by those gathered as they speak the line.

One: Like the roots of a strong oak,

(Hands held out in front, palms down)

All: **Like the roots of a strong oak,**

One: God is under our feet.

All: **God is under our feet.**

One: Like the stars in the night sky,

(Hands over head, with fingers gently wiggling)

All: **Like the stars in the night sky,**

One: God is over our heads.

All: **God is over our heads.**

One: Like the sun on the horizon,

(Right arm held straight out, with hand at a 90 degree angle, palm away from body. Left hand is held, palm up, under the right, to form the "horizon".)

All: **Like the sun on the horizon,**

One: God is ever before us.

All: **God is ever before us.**

One: Like the gentle rain falling,

(Hands are brought towards face, palms toward body, fingers gently wiggling, and lowered until they are in front of the heart.)

All: **Like the gentle rain falling,**

One: God's love is filling our hearts.

All: **God's love is filling our hearts.**

One: Like the wings of an eagle,

(Arms outstretched on either side)

All: **Like the wings of an eagle,**

One: We open our arms to care for this world.

All: **We open our arms to care for this world.**

One: Like the river which runs to the ocean,

(Place palms together, fingers pointing away from body. Allow hands to meander from the right to the left in front of the body, imitating the course of a river.)

All: Like the river which runs to the ocean,

One: We know that our home is in God.

All: We know that our home is in God.

One: And so we go forth

(Take the hands of those on either side)

All: And so we go forth

One: Surrounded by the presence of God,

All: Surrounded by the presence of God,

One: And filled with the peace of God. Amen.

(Raise hands up together)

All: And filled with the peace of God. Amen.

Naming Strengths

Spirited Lives

Gathering

One: Bold lives roll stones of resistance away,
And the vision receives breath.

All: Rejoice in the courage that sets us free!

One: Spirited lives part seas of rigid ways,
And justice dances away from slavery.

All: Rejoice in the courage that sets us free!

One: Daring lives break shackles of intimidation,
And truth speaks with no constraint.

All: Rejoice in the courage that sets us free!

One: Persevering lives tear down walls of greed
And life in abundance is no longer a dream.

All: Rejoice in the courage that sets us free!

Song: Praise with Joy the World's Creator

Readings

John 18:19-23

Then the high priest questioned Jesus about his disciples and about his teaching. Jesus answered, "I have spoken openly to the world; I have always taught in synagogues and in the temple, where all the Jews come together. I have said nothing in secret. Why do you ask me? Ask those who heard what I said to them; they know what I said." When he had said this, one of the police standing nearby struck Jesus on the face, saying, "Is that how you answer the high priest?" Jesus answered, "If I have spoken wrongly, testify to the wrong. But if I have spoken rightly, why do you strike me?"

Esther 3:8-9a, 11, 13; 4:4a, 10-16; 5:1-3; 7:3

Haman said to King Ahasuerus, "There is a certain people scattered and separated among the peoples in all the provinces of your land; their laws are different from those of every other people, and they do not keep the king's laws, so that it is not appropriate for the king to tolerate them. If it pleases the king, let a decree be issued for their destruction." ... And the king said to Haman... "The people are given to you to do with as seems good to you." ... And letters were sent to all the king's provinces, giving orders to destroy all Jews, young and old, women and children on the thirteenth day of the twelfth month... and to plunder their goods... When Esther's maids and her eunuchs came and told her, the queen was deeply distressed... and she sent a message to her relative Mordecai, saying, "All the king's servants and the people of the king's provinces know that if any man or woman goes to the king without being called, there is but one law — all alike are to be put to death. Only if the king holds out the golden scepter to someone, may that person live." ... Mordecai sent a reply to Esther, saying, "Do not think that in the king's palace you will escape any more than all the other Jews... Who knows? Perhaps you have come to royal dignity for just such a time as this." Then Esther sent a reply, saying, "Go, gather all the Jews... and hold a fast for three days on my behalf. I and my maids will also fast as you do. After that I will go to the king." ... On the third day Esther put on her royal robes and stood in the inner court of the king's palace... As soon as the king saw Queen Esther standing in the court, he held out to her the golden scepter that was in his hand. Then Esther approached and touched the top of the scepter. The king said to her, "What is it, Queen Esther? What is your request? It shall be given to you, even to the half of my land... Queen Esther answered, "If I have won your favour, O king, and if it pleases the king, let my life be given me — that is my petition — and the lives of my people — that is my request."

Psalm 27:14
Be strong, and let your heart take courage.

Response

Prayer

God of Blessing,

Clear as the resounding ocean,

So may our words be.

Certain as the sun in its path,

So may our persistence be.

Soaring as the ancient mountains,

So may our courage be.

Abundant as the life-giving air,

So may our faith be.

Amen.

Song: God is Passionate Life

Have Salt in Yourselves

Preparation: *Papers with each person's name on the top, pens for writing for each person, small bowl or container of salt.*

Gathering

One: Scattering seeds on varied soil,
A sower plants with faith.

All: **Hands open, gifts offered:**
This is how we salt the earth.

One: Patience in seeking that which was lost,
A woman sweeps with hope.

All: **Hands open, gifts offered:**
This is how we salt the earth.

One: Binding a roadside stranger's wounds
A man responds in love.

All: **Hands open, gifts offered:**

This is how we salt the earth.

One: Living a vision of justice and mercy,

Christ invites others to follow.

All: **Hands open, gifts offered:**

This is how we salt the earth.

 As a Fire is Meant for Burning

Readings

Numbers 18:9, 19
Every offering of theirs that they render to me is a most holy thing... and all the holy offerings that the people present to me... are as a covenant of salt.

1 Corinthians 12:4-12
Now there are a variety of gifts, but the same Spirit; and there are varieties of services... and activities, but it is the same God who activates all of them in everyone. To each is given the manifestation of the Spirit for the common good. To one is given the utterance of wisdom, and to another the utterance of knowledge, to another faith, to another gifts of healing, to another the working of miracles, and to another a prophetic voice... All of these are activated by one and the same Spirit.

Mark 9:50b
Have salt in yourselves, and be at peace with one another.

Matthew 5:13
You are the salt of the earth.

Salty Gifts

The leader explains that just as salt gives flavour, so it is with our gifts. Each of the distinct gifts that we offer adds flavours to the life around us. Participants are then invited to name the gifts that they see in the lives of each of those in the gathering. This can happen either verbally, or by writing the affirmations on papers which are passed around with each person's name on top. If this is done verbally, with each person's gifts being named one at a time, then at the end of the affirmations, that person is presented with a small bowl or container of salt, and the group says, " (Name), *the salt of your living is a blessing to all." If the affirmations are done on paper, then this blessing can simply be done around the circle after everyone has received the paper with their own name on it.*

Prayer

One: Gracious One,

We offer common blessings

In our daily living:

A gesture of strength,

A word of daring,

A prayer of kindness.

All: **These, the tidings of our faith.**

One: We shape the tone and texture
Of how your vision is realized:
Weaving threads of justice,
Composing psalms of healing,
Sculpting contours of wisdom.

All: **These, the tidings of our faith.**

One: We continue the holy story
With chapters of our own:
One life offering witness,
Another speaking as prophet,
Another walking as disciple;
Each one part of the whole.

All: **These, the tidings of our faith.**
Amen.

Song: Heaven is Singing for Joy

Greenwood of Wisdom

Gathering

One: When we let the seed fall
Into the good soil of our spirits:

All: God's greenwood of wisdom rises once again.

One: When we receive God's banquet welcome
Into the void of our uncertainties:

All: God's greenwood of wisdom rises once again.

One: When we gleam like a hillside city
Into the sham of hidden tyrannies:

All: God's greenwood of wisdom rises once again.

One: When we bind the wounds of intolerance
Into a balm of kind relations:

All: God's greenwood of wisdom rises once again.

Song: Who Comes from God

Matthew 13:54

Jesus came to his hometown and began to teach the people in their synagogue, so that they were astounded and said, "Where did this man get this wisdom?"

Proverbs 3:13-15, 17-18a

Happy are those who find wisdom, and those who get understanding, for her income is better than silver, and her revenue better than gold. She is more precious than jewels, and nothing can compare with her... Her ways are ways of pleasantness, and all her paths are peace. She is a tree of life to all those who hold on to her.

James 3:13

Who is wise and understanding among you? Show by your life that your works are done with gentleness born of wisdom.

The Wisdom of Solomon 7:22-28

There is in wisdom a spirit that is intelligent, holy, unique, manifold, subtle, mobile, clear, unpolluted, distinct, invulnerable, loving the good, keen, irresistible, beneficent, humane, steadfast, sure, free from anxiety, all-powerful, overseeing all, and penetrating through all spirits that are intelligent, pure, and altogether subtle. For wisdom is more mobile than any motion; because of her pureness she pervades and penetrates all things. For she is a breath of the power of God, and a pure emanation of the glory of God... she is a reflection of eternal light, a spotless mirror of the working of God, and an image of God's goodness... In every generation she passes into holy souls and makes them friends of God, and prophets; for God loves nothing so much as the person who lives with wisdom.

Response

Wisdom's Psalm

We scatter our decisions and days
With trifles and met expectations;
All the while, longing for the blaze and ember
Of bushes set on fire,
Or angels filling the sky with song.

We subdue the expanse of faith
Into prescribed meetings and lethargic institutions;
All the while, yearning for the spark and luster
Of sunbeams flooding into empty tombs,
Or fiery pillars leading to liberation.

Even so, she is present.
All the wild reasonings of authority
Cannot quell her shining.

Like diamonds of light

Dancing through the leaves

She beckons us to breathe Life in again.

Song: O God of Matchless Glory

Gathering At Table

This Good Journey

A communion service for the home

Gathering

One: God be with us on every journey.

All: **Amen.**

Prayer

One: God of abundant life:

We gather around this table

As part of your beloved creation.

We thank you for your many gifts to us:

For clouds and sky,

for plants and soil, mountains and oceans;

For all creatures of the air,

for all creatures of the land;

For all creatures of the water

that we share this world with;

For sending us so many sisters and brothers

To share this good journey with.

Other thanksgivings may be added.

God of many blessings,

As we gather around this table,

May we feel the strength of your love for us.

All: Amen.

Celebrating the Sharing of Bread

Readings

Exodus 16:1, 4a, 5, 13b-17, 31

The people of Israel came into the wilderness... after they had departed from the land of Egypt... Then God said to Moses, "I am going to rain bread from heaven for you, and each day the people shall go out and gather enough for that day... On the sixth day, when they prepare what they bring in, it will be twice as much as they gather on other days in preparation for the Sabbath." ... In the morning there was a layer of dew around the camp. When the layer of dew lifted, there on the surface of the wilderness was a fine flaky substance, as fine as frost on the ground. When the Israelites saw it, they said to one another, "What is it?" For they did not know what it was. Moses said to them, "It is the bread that God has given you to eat. This is what God has commanded: 'Gather as much of it as each of you needs, providing an equal amount for each person in your tent.'" The Israelites did so, some gathering more, some less... The people of Israel called this daily food manna.

John 6:5, 8-14

When Jesus looked up and saw a large crowd coming toward him, he said... "Where are we to buy bread for these people to eat?" ... One of his disciples, Andrew... said to him, "There is a boy here who has five barley loaves and two fish. But what are they among so many people?" Jesus said, "Have the people sit down." Now there was a great deal of grass in the place; so they sat down, about five thousand in all. Then Jesus took the loaves, and when he had given thanks, he distributed then to those who were seated; so also the fish, as much as they wanted. When they were satisfied, he told his disciples, "Gather up the fragments left over, so that nothing may be lost." So they gathered them up, and from the fragments of the five barley loaves, left by those who had eaten, they filled twelve baskets. When the people saw the sign that he had done, they began to say, "This is indeed the prophet who is to come into the world."

Prayer

One: *(Holding up bread)*

Jesus taught that bread was meant to be shared,

and that all are welcome at God's table.

Jesus asked to be remembered in the sharing of the bread.

All: **In this sharing,**

In this welcoming,

In this remembering,

We celebrate the gift of life.

Bread is shared around the table.

Celebrating the Sharing of the Cup

Readings

Psalm 104:1-2, 3b, 5, 13, 15, 24a

Bless God, O my soul. You are clothed with honour and majesty, and wrapped in light as with a robe. You stretch out the heavens like a tent... you make the clouds your chariot, gliding on the wings of the wind. You fixed the earth on its foundations, for ever and ever it shall not be shaken... From your high halls you water the mountains, satisfying the earth with the fruit of your works... You bring forth the fruit of the vine to make our hearts glad... and the bread of the earth to give our hearts strength... How countless are your works, O God!

John 15:5, 9, 12, 11

Jesus said to them, "I am the vine, you are the branches. Those who abide in me and I in them bear much fruit... As God has loved me, so I have loved you; abide in my love... This is my commandment, that you love one another as I have loved you... I have said these things to you so that my joy may be in you, and that your joy may be complete."

Prayer

One: *(Holding up pitcher)*

Jesus taught that all of life is woven together,

and that love is why we're here.

Jesus asked to be remembered in the sharing of the cup.

All: **In this weaving together,**

In this loving,

In this remembering,

We celebrate the gift of life.

Each one pours from the pitcher into the cup of the person next to them and when the pitcher has gone around the table, everyone drinks from their cup.

Blessing

One: May there be bread for the journey,

May there be friends along the way,

May we dare to dream and laugh and love,

And seek justice every day.

May God's presence give us wisdom,

May God's presence grant us peace,

May God's be the hand that gives us strength,

May we hope in the promised Feast.

All: **Amen.**

All share in a meal together.

This Holy Time

A home communion service for special celebrations

Preparation: *A focal point or centrepiece to mark the special occasion should be arranged in the centre of the table before this service begins. For example, if it is a person's birthday being celebrated, photos of the person at different stages of life may be arranged. If it is a wedding anniversary, wedding photos or momentos may be placed in the centre.*

Gathering

One: May God be in our hearts and in our home.

All: **Amen.**

Prayer

One: Glorious Creator,

We celebrate our lives and this world.

We are blessed by so many gifts:

This circle of loved ones,

and those far and wide.

This food for our sharing,
and those who provide it.

This place we name home,
and all the memories here.

This earth filled with beauty,
and all life that surrounds us.

This time, which you give us
to flourish in your love.

We rejoice in this abundance
and give thanks for your grace.

Other prayers of thanksgiving may be offered.

Spirit of Love,
Fill our hearts with delight
and our moments with wonder
as we gather to celebrate
the blessing of (*special occasion is named*).

May this special time we share

Fill us with warmth and with joy.

All: **Amen.**

Sharing of Stories

One or several stories are shared around the table. For instance, if this is a birthday, stories about the person could be shared. Or, if it is a holiday, memories from previous celebrations could be shared. Another option is to read a particular story that is meaningful for the occasion.

Readings

ECCLESIASTES 9:7, 9
Eat your bread with enjoyment and share your cup with delight, for you have God's favour... Enjoy life with the ones you love all the days that are given to you under the sun.

JOHN 6:35A
Jesus said to them, "I am the bread of life."

JOHN 15:5
Jesus said to them, "I am the vine, you are the branches. Those who abide in me and I in them bear much fruit."

PSALM 36:7-9
How precious is your steadfast love, O God! All people... feast on the abundance of your house, and you give them drink from the river of your delights. For with you is the fountain of life.

Prayer for the Sharing of the Bread and the Cup

One: God is with us.

God takes delight in our delight.

May we give thanks for this holy presence.

May we give thanks for this holy time.

Gathered here, we remember all our special moments.

Gathered here, we remember all who walk in faith.

Gathered here, we remember the banquet

that Jesus asked us all to share.

(Holding up bread)

This is the bread of joy.

This is the bread of wisdom.

This is the bread of hope.

Gifts offered in love and tenderness.

(Pour from pitcher into cup, and then hold up cup)

This is the cup of grace.

This is the cup of compassion.

This is the cup of strength.

Gifts offered in love and tenderness.

Let us share and delight in these gifts to us.

The bread and pitcher are passed around the table, and each shares with the person seated next to them.

Blessing

One: God of love,

With open hands, we have received,

All: With open hands, we have received.

One: With open hearts, may we now share.

All: With open hearts, may we now share.

One: And may your peace fill our home and our world.

All: And may your peace fill our home and our world. Amen.

All share in a meal together.

Our Hearts Remember

To mark the anniversary of a loss of a loved one

Preparation: *Each person is invited to bring an item which symbolizes what they remember most about the loved one. A time for sharing these remembrances will take place after the readings. A picture of the person being remembered is placed on a table in the middle of those gathered. There should be enough room on the table for everyone to place their symbols.*

Gathering

One: God of Compassion,
We gather in recognition of a life
That touched our own.

All: **Our hearts remember the days that were shared.**
Our hearts remember the love that was given.

One: Memories have accompanied us in this time,
Reminding us of so much received,
And so much lost.

All: **Our hearts remember the days that were shared.**

Our hearts remember the love that was given.

One: Each has journeyed this path of loss,

Accepting comfort in varied ways.

All: **Our hearts remember the days that were shared.**

Our hearts remember the love that was given.

One: Our love for *(name)* will not be diminished.

The gifts *(name)* shared will always remain.

All: **Our hearts remember the days that were shared.**

Our hearts remember the love that was given.

Readings

John 11:33-36

When Jesus saw Mary weeping, and the Jews who came with her also weeping, he was greatly disturbed in spirit and deeply moved. He said, "Where have you laid Lazarus?" They said to him, "Come and see." And Jesus began to weep. So the Jews said, "See how he loved him!"

2 Corinthians 1:3-4

Blessed be the God of mercy and of all consolation, who comforts us in our sorrows, so that we can offer others, in their sorrows, the consolation that we ourselves have received.

Romans 8:38-39
I am convinced that there is nothing in death or life, in the world as it is, or the world as it shall be, nothing in all of creation, that can separate us from the love of God in Christ.

Other readings/poetry may be shared.

Sharing of Memories

Each person shares their symbol, why it reminds them of the loved one, and places it on the table.

Prayer

God of Our Hope,

We hold these stories

With gentle hands:

Knowing their joy,

Learning their loss,

Returning to them again and again

To seek mending and meaning.

We share these stories

With full hearts:

Revealing their treasures,

Confessing their ache,

Hopeful that this keeping of memory

Will bring peace again.

Amen.

Sharing of Music

If the person being remembered had a favourite piece of music, it might be played or sung at this time.

A meal is shared among those gathered.

It Is Good

A service of thanksgiving for the home

Preparation: *Candles are set on the table for each one gathered there, as well as a central candle for the very centre of the table.*

Gathering

One: *(as centre candle is lit)*

May we share the light and love of God.

All: **Amen.**

Each one lights their candle from the central candle, and sets it on the table.

Readings

GENESIS 1:31

And when God had finished creating the heavens and the earth, God saw everything that had been made, and, indeed, it was very good.

All: **And God said, "It is good, it is very good."**

Psalm 100
Make a joyful noise to God, all the earth. Worship God with gladness... for God created us and we are God's people.

All: **And God said, "It is good, it is very good."**

Prayer

One: Each day, O God,
We receive so much that is good:
A rainbow of colours,
A symphony of sounds,
A banquet of flavours,
A bouquet of aromas.

As the seasons turn,
We receive again:
The crunch of amber leaves underfoot,
The fragrance of cut grass in the sun,
The warmth of soup when snow is falling,
The first crocus to appear from the cold ground.

As moments come,

As moments go,

We receive even more:

The song of a sparrow to lift our hearts,

The smile of a friend to set things right,

The grace of a deer to fill us with wonder,

The laughter and love shared around this table.

For all we have received, O God,

We say with you, "It is very good,"

And we give you grateful hearts in return.

All: **Amen.**

Sharing of Stories

Each person around the table is invited to share a story about something that they experienced that day/week that they are thankful for.

Blessing

One: Our living is a blessing:

All: **And so we give God thanks.**

One: Our loved ones are a blessing:

All: **And so we give God thanks.**

One: This earth is a blessing:

All: And so we give God thanks.

One: This meal we share,

This time we share,

Is, indeed, a blessing:

All: And so we give God thanks.

Amen.

A meal is shared together.

Taking Heart

Wings of Strength

Preparation: *A basket filled with enough origami birds for each person present.*

Gathering

One: This is the wilderness time,
when every path is obscure
and thorns have grown around words of hope.

All: **Be the wings of our strength, O God,**
in this time of wilderness waiting.

One: This is the time of stone, not bread,
when even the sunrise feels uncertain
and everything tastes of bitterness.

All: **Be the wings of our strength, O God,**
in this time of wilderness waiting.

One: This is the time of ashes and dust,
when darkness clothes our dreams
and no star shines a guiding light.

All: **Be the wings of our strength, O God,**
in this time of wilderness waiting.

One: This is the time of treading life,
waiting for the swells to subside
and for the chaos to clear.

All: **Be the wings of our strength, O God,**
in this time of wilderness waiting.

Song: Wellspring of Wisdom

Readings

GENESIS 21:9-10, 14-16

Sarah saw the son of Hagar the Egyptian, whom she had borne to Abraham, playing with her son Isaac. So she said to Abraham, "Cast out this slave woman with her son; for the son of this slave woman shall not inherit along with my son Isaac." ... So Abraham rose early in the morning, and took bread and a skin of water, and gave it to Hagar, putting it on her shoulder, along with the child, and sent her away. And she departed, and wandered about in the wilderness of Beer-sheba. When the water in the skin was gone, she placed the child under one of the bushes. Then she went and sat down opposite him a good way off... for she said, "Do not let me look on the death of this child." And as she sat opposite him, she lifted up her voice and wept.

All: **My heart is in anguish within me.**

And I say, "O, that I had wings like a dove!

I would fly away and be at rest." (Psalm 55:4a, 6)

Matthew 2:13-14

An angel of God appeared to Joseph in a dream and said, "Get up, take Mary and the child, and flee to Egypt, and remain there until I tell you; for Herod is about to search for the child, to destroy him." Then Joseph got up, took Mary and the child by night, and went to Egypt.

All: **My heart is in anguish within me.**

And I say, "O, that I had wings like a dove!

I would fly away and be at rest."

Genesis 32:11, 22-25

And Jacob said, "O God, deliver me, I pray, from the hand of my brother Esau, for I am afraid of him; he may come and kill us all... That same night he got up and took his family and crossed the ford of the Jabbok. He took them and sent them across the stream, and likewise everything that he had. And Jacob was left alone. Then, someone wrestled with him through the night until daybreak.

All: **My heart is in anguish within me.**

And I say, "O, that I had wings like a dove!

I would fly away and be at rest."

GENESIS 21:17-19

And God heard the voice of Hagar and her son; and an angel of God called to Hagar and said to her, "What troubles you, Hagar? Do not be afraid; for God has heard you. Come, lift up your son, and hold him close, for God will make a great nation of him." Then God opened her eyes and she saw a well of water. She went, and filled the skin with water, and gave her son a drink.

All: Those who hope in God will renew their strength,

They shall soar with wings like the eagle's.

(Isaiah 40:31)

MATTHEW 2:19-21

When Herod died, an angel of God appeared in a dream to Joseph in Egypt and said, "Get up, take Mary and the child, and go to the land of Israel, for those who were seeking the child's life are dead." Then Joseph got up, took Mary and the child, and went to the land of Israel.

All: Those who hope in God will renew their strength,

They shall soar with wings like the eagle's.

GENESIS 32:26-28; 33:1, 3-4, 10B

The one that Jacob wrestled with said to him, "Let me go, for the day is breaking." But Jacob said, "I will not let you go, unless you bless me." So the other said to him, "What is your name?" And he replied, "Jacob." Then the other said, "You shall no longer be called Jacob, but Israel, for you have striven with God and with mortals." And Jacob received his blessing... Then Jacob looked up and saw Esau coming, and four hundred men with him... he went ahead of his family, bowing to the ground seven times until he came near his brother. But Esau ran to meet him, and embraced him, and fell on his neck and kissed him, and they wept... Then Jacob said to Esau... "Truly to see your face is like seeing the face of God — since you have received me with so much favour."

All: **Those who hope in God will renew their strength,**
They shall soar with wings like the eagle's.

Response

A Time of Reflection

A basket of folded origami birds is passed around the group. As each person takes one from the basket, they are invited to answer this question: What are the wings of strength you need at this time in your own life?

Prayer

One: Gracious Spirit,
When the dry wind of confusion
Fills our every breath;
When the shadows of fear
Echo every step,

All: **Restore our hearts into hope**
That we might seek a good path.

One: When every door
Seems locked up tight;
When every thought
Seems weighted down,

All: **Restore our hearts into hope**
That we might seek a good path.

One: When the sheltering ground
Turns unstable and entangled;
When the nourishing streams
Turn hostile and arid,

All: **Restore our hearts into hope**
That we might seek a good path.
Amen.

Song: The Lone, Wild Bird

Heart of God

Gathering

One: There is a world that weeps,
yearning for a sign of mercy.

All: **The heart of God within us has no hands but our own.**

One: There is a friend in anguish
Besieged by unexpected pain.

All: **The heart of God within us has no ears but our own.**

One: There is a multitude harmed and weary
From prejudicial ways.

All: **The heart of God within us has no eyes but our own.**

One: A stranger faces death alone
Wondering if anyone will remember.

All: **The heart of God within us has no tears but our own.**

One: There is a life, hollow and lonely,
Longing for someone to walk alongside.

All: **The heart of God within us has no feet but our own.**

Song: Mother and God

Readings

Luke 7:11-13
Jesus went to a town called Nain, and his disciples and a large crowd went with him. As he approached the gate of the town, a man who had died was being carried out. He was his mother's only son, and she was a widow; and with her was a large crowd from the town. When Jesus saw her, he had compassion for her.

Leviticus 19:33-34, 18
When strangers reside with you in your land, you shall not oppress them. The stranger who resides with you shall be to you as the citizen among you... for you were once strangers in the land of Egypt... and you shall love your neighbor as yourself.

Exodus 2:5-6
The daughter of Pharoah came down to bathe at the river, while her attendants walked beside the river. She saw the basket among the reeds and sent her maid to bring it. When she opened it, she saw the child. He was crying, and she took pity on him.

Luke 10:29-36
And the lawyer asked Jesus, "Who is my neighbor?" Jesus replied, "A man was going down from Jerusalem to Jericho, and fell into the hands of robbers, who stripped him, beat him, and went away, leaving him half dead. Now by chance a priest was going down that road; and when he saw him, he passed by on the other side. So likewise a Levite, when he came to the place and saw him, passed by on the other side. But a Samaritan while traveling came near him; and when he saw him, he was moved with pity. He went to him and bandaged his wounds, having poured oil and wine on them. Then he put him on his own animal, brought him to an inn, and took care of him. The next day he took out two denarii, gave them to the innkeeper, and said, 'Take care of him; and when I come back, I will repay you whatever more you spend.' Which of these three, do you think, was a neighbor to the man who fell into the hands of the robbers?"

Luke 6:36
Be compassionate, just as God is compassionate.

Song: We are Pilgrims

Prayer of Compassion

Participants are invited to name out loud those they have concern for after each petition.

One: Source of Our Love:

You journey with us,

Offering endless compassion

And enduring visions.

Hear our prayers
As we seek to join with you
In weaving patterns of healing and hope
Wherever the fabric of life is torn.
We pray for all
Whose lives are diminished
By difficulty, suffering or loss
We name them before you now:
For those in need of healing...
For those facing difficulty...
For those suffering from injustice...
For those seeking courage...
For those harmed by violence...
For those in sorrow...
For others we name before you now...

All: **May strength be theirs.**
May comfort be theirs.
May love uphold them.
May we, in turn
Reveal compassion to them
In our words and our ways.

A time of silence for those gathered to reflect on how they might reach out to those named in the prayers.

One: Source of Our Mercy:
Journey with us now
As we seek to walk
Your path of blessing.
Amen.

Song: Though I May Speak

Blessing

All: **As we go from here,**
May our every action proclaim our hope
in justice;
May our every word proclaim our joy
in compassion;
May our every heartbeat proclaim our peace
in God.
Amen.

Peace, Frenzied Spirit

Preparation: *Paper and pens for each person present.*

Gathering

One: Waves of demands wash over us,
Tossing us into chaos.

All: **And a voice calls out, "Peace, frenzied spirit."**

One: Snares of necessity intercept us,
Binding us in anxiety.

All: **And a voice calls out, "Peace, frenzied spirit."**

One: Fumes of uncertainty circle round us,
Smothering us with distrust.

All: **And a voice calls out, "Peace, frenzied spirit."**

One: Gusts of expectation roar through us,

Pounding us into distraction.

All: **And a voice calls out, "Peace, frenzied spirit."**

Song: Spirit of Life

MATTHEW 11:28
Jesus said, "Come unto me, all you that are weary and carrying heavy burdens, and I will give you rest."

DEUTERONOMY 30:10B, 11-14
Return to God with all your heart and soul. God's word... is not beyond your reach. It is not in heaven, so that you need wonder, "Who will go up to heaven for us and bring it down to us, so that we can hear and practice it?" Nor is it beyond the seas, so that you need to wonder, "Who will cross the seas for us and bring it back to us, so that we can hear and practice it?" No, the word is very near to you; it is in your mouth and your heart for you to perceive.

PSALM 46:10
Be still and know that I am God.

LUKE 5:15-16
Now more than ever the word about Jesus spread abroad; many crowds would gather to hear him and to be cured of their diseases. And Jesus would withdraw to deserted places and pray.

ISAIAH 30:15
In returning and rest you shall find salvation; in quietness and in trust you shall find your strength.

Response

Time for Reflection

Each person is invited to reflect on what aspects of their life are most life-giving, particularly in times when they feel the pull of many demands. Participants are asked to list seven of these aspects on a piece of paper. The group is then invited into triads, where they discuss whatever they noticed about the lists that they came up with.

Prayer

God of Life,

Like a promised land,

You invite us to leave our frantic ways.

Like a banquet-laden table,

You bid us to restore our empty spirits.

Like a pool of still waters,

You call us to cease our crowded living.

Like a bright and shining star,

You lead us,

And restore our lives of wonder.

Amen.

Song: Come and Find the Quiet Centre

Song Index

VU *Voices United: The Hymn and Worship Book of the United Church of Canada*, John Ambrose, ed. (Etobicoke, Ontario: The United Church Publishing House, 1996).

Scripture Index

Old Testament

Apocrypha

New Testament

Notes

Notes

Notes

Also by Keri K. Wehlander

Courage for Hallelujahs
Alternate Worship Resources for Lent and Easter
Keri. K. Wehlander, editor
This creative and refreshing volume provides life-affirming resources for Lent and Easter. Authors from across Canada have contributed a wide variety of prayers, meditations, litanies, intergenerational events and worship services. Insightful and eloquent, these resources will benefit all those seeking new ways of approaching these seasons in our communities of faith.

1-55134-083-6 paperback $15.95

Joy is our Banquet
Resources for Everyday Worship
Keri K. Wehlander
Worship planners for small groups, retreats, committee meetings, or special events will find this a timely and uplifting liturgical resource. Complete with prayers, litanies, song suggestions, and biblical passages, these devotions may be readily adapted for use in Sunday morning or other large group worship settings, or for personal use. The refreshing, sometimes startling images affirm everyday experiences as integral to all that is holy. Poetic and accessible, *Joy is our Banquet* will nurture the spiritual journey of all who draw from it.

1-55134-050-X paperback $14.95

About the Author

Circles of Grace is Keri's third book with The United Church Publishing House. Her first book, *Joy is our Banquet* became a UCPH best-seller within weeks of its release in 1996. Keri's next project was to edit a collection of life-affirming resources for Lent and Easter called *Courage for Hallelujahs* (see previous page for more details about these books).

Keri's other previously published materials include: "Spring Blossoms" in the March 1997 *Observer*; "The Road Less Travelled," a series of Bible studies (as well as photography done by Keri), appearing in 1994 in *Esprit* (a Lutheran women's publication); "Go and Tell What You Have Seen and Heard," a general worship outline for the Decade, and "The Stones Cry Out," a worship outline on women and violence, both published in *Mandate—Special Edition* (Women and Men in Dialogue); and "Who Will Roll Away the Stone?" a Bible study in the Winter 1990 edition of *Exchange*.

Keri lives in British Columbia with her partner, Curtis, and enjoys long walks on the beach (with time for beachcombing), conversations shared with good friends, reading poetry, and home-style Mexican cooking.